PRINCETON STUDIES IN INTERNATIONAL FINANCE NO. 22

External Surpluses, Capital Flows, and Credit Policy in the European Economic Community, 1958 to 1967

by

Samuel I. Katz

INTERNATIONAL FINANCE SECTION

DEPARTMENT OF ECONOMICS

PRINCETON UNIVERSITY

PRINCETON, NEW JERSEY

1969

Printed in the United States of America by Princeton University Press
at Princeton, New Jersey

CONTENTS

LIST OF TABLES

EXTERNAL SURPLUSES, CAPITAL FLOWS, AND CREDIT POLICY IN THE EUROPEAN ECONOMIC COMMUNITY, 1958 TO 1967

I. INNOVATIONS IN THE TECHNOLOGY OF CENTRAL BANKING

After 1958, when European currencies became convertible, two economic developments—unexpectedly large balance-of-payments surpluses between 1958 and 1962 and the growth in international flows of private capital—threatened to undermine the effectiveness of actions by the central banks in meeting their goals of domestic stabilization in the countries of the European Economic Community. Because of these developments, the European banks were confronted with a conflict between the requirements for domestic and for international balance. Under these conditions, measures to restore domestic balance were likely to add to the external-payments surplus; on the other hand, policies that helped to reduce the external surpluses were likely to accelerate advances in domestic prices and costs.

The stubbornness of this policy dilemma, and the sudden spurt in exports between 1957 and 1958, led some Europeans to link their current-account surpluses to inflationary conditions elsewhere. In their view, the persistent creep in European prices and costs after 1958 came to be regarded as a manifestation of "imported inflation," attributable to the failure of important trading partners—in particular, the United States—to discipline adequately their international spending. The continuing payments deficits of the United States came to be regarded by some as the primary source of Europe's imported inflation.

It soon became evident that the payments surpluses had introduced important limitations on the employment of credit policy for domestic goals. The central banks' control over the credit base was seriously threatened by the liquidity created when the authorities were obliged to purchase incoming foreign currencies from the customers of the commercial banks. Efforts to sterilize these additions to internal liquidity through the traditional tools of monetary control (discount policy, uniform reserve requirements, and—on the restricted scale common to these countries—open-market operations) raised questions

1

about the capacities of European financial markets to absorb offsetting operations as well as about the powers and range of policy tools available to the central banks.

Equally important, the enhanced mobility of private capital meant that measures of general monetary restraint could in many cases be self-defeating. By helping to push domestic interest-rate levels above those in foreign centers, such measures merely created incentives for additional inflows of private capital—adding to the reserve accruals which the central banks were obliged to purchase.

Greater mobility of capital within Europe was inevitable after 1958 with convertibility attained, restrictions dismantled, and financial markets more closely integrated, both among the countries in the Common Market and between them and the rest of the world. But several other developments at that time added greatly to intercountry flows of capital. Because rates were often lower there than in domestic markets, the growth of the Euro-dollar market encouraged European exporters and importers to switch from domestic to foreign-currency credits for ordinary business financing, especially as the volume of their foreign trade expanded and their credit-worthiness improved. This willingness to borrow foreign currencies for domestic requirements was also stimulated by a growing rigidity in exchange-rate policy among the major industrial nations, both within the European Economic Community and among the Group of Ten. As changes in exchange-rate parities became less and less likely, European businessmen became increasingly prepared to borrow in foreign currencies—especially where the rate was cheaper—and even to maintain uncovered positions on the credits in order to save the cost of forward cover.

In this environment, the volume of flows of private capital expanded rapidly after 1958. More important perhaps, the threat of additional flows if the financial authorities raised domestic rates above those abroad became a major consideration in European decisions about the extent, the timing, and the particular instruments of credit restraint in each country. The broad range of capital flows which actually took place in Europe can be identified under five principal headings:[1]

(a) Short-term funds—responsive to interest differentials, both with and, on occasion, speculatively without forward exchange cover,

[1] These categories, though analytically distinct, may overlap in practice. For example, "commercial credits" could also be included in some cases under "precautionary and speculative flows."

(b) Commercial credits—obtained by European entrepreneurs in foreign currencies, either directly or through local institutions,

(c) Fixed-interest securities, equities, and convertible debentures—purchased privately, either in foreign currencies or in foreign centers or both,

(d) Precautionary and speculative flows—including "leads and lags" in foreign-trade financing, prompted either by interest differentials or by uncertainties about the stability of an exchange-rate parity,[2]

(e) Direct investment flows—financed in foreign (European or Euro-dollar) currencies.

EXTERNAL LIQUIDITY AND DOMESTIC CREDIT POLICY

Given this enhanced mobility of capital, the central banks of the European Economic Community could not hope to make credit restraint effective in a period of payments surpluses unless they could devise ways to sterilize the excess domestic liquidity created by those surpluses without at the same time provoking unwanted inflows of private capital. Some economists had maintained that these two objectives could not be reconciled in a system of fixed exchange rates; that, in a period of continuing payments surpluses, "The Central Bank is bound to lose control of the money supply, and therefore over the level of total spending."[3]

Even if the central bank could "for a time at least, prevent the secondary deposit expansion by the commercial banks," Lutz was convinced that the banking system was bound to acquire "sufficient cash to support the *primary* deposit expansion which derives directly from the sales to them of foreign exchange by their customers." Scott and Schmidt were more optimistic: "Both the potential primary and secondary expansions . . . could be prevented through open market sales," a conclusion subsequently challenged, in part on technical

[2] Precautionary and speculative flows of funds directly related to the timing and locale of foreign-trade financing in Europe are described—and indications of the volume of the flows in Europe during the 1950s are roughly suggested—in my papers, "Leads and Lags in Sterling Payments," *Review of Economics and Statistics*, Vol. XXXV (February 1953) and *Sterling Speculation and European Convertibility: 1955-1958*, Essays in International Finance No. 37 (Princeton, N.J.: International Finance Section, 1961); and in Paul Einzig, "What Are Leads and Lags?" *Banca Nazionale del Lavoro Quarterly Review*, No. 83 (December 1967), pp. 376-389.

[3] Friedrich A. Lutz, *International Payments and Monetary Policy in the World Today*, Wicksell Lectures, 1961 (Stockholm: Almquist and Wiksell, 1961), p. 37.

grounds, by Oppenheimer and Lutz.[4] Lutz was convinced that the central bank's task was hopeless: "Reserve requirements will reach their maximum level, the stock of open-market paper will run out and the consequently unhindered expansion in commercial bank liquidity will render the official rediscount rate ineffective."[5]

The early experiences within the Common Market seemed to support a pessimistic judgment. The German central bank raised reserve requirements five times between mid-1959 and mid-1960, but this aggressive tactic failed to restore the Bundesbank's control over the internal credit base. On the contrary, disequilibrating inflows of capital, provoked by the tight monetary policy, finally forced the German authorities to change that policy late in 1960; ultimately, the DM was revalued in early 1961. Similarly, inflows of capital into the Netherlands convinced Roosa that "tight money has not . . . been the sole and satisfactory answer" and led him to conclude that "the days of simple reliance upon monetary policy . . . may possibly be gone forever."[6]

But these misgivings proved, in the end, to be exaggerated. The European monetary authorities were not prepared to abdicate their primary responsibility to promote domestic economic objectives. They accepted the limitations on their freedom of action imposed by the system of fixed exchange rates and proceeded to develop—gradually and even on occasion through a disorderly process of trial and error—policy instruments that would enable them to regain control over internal credit availabilities. As a result, monetary policy bore the major burden for domestic stabilization in these countries between 1958 and 1967, frequently with only limited support from fiscal policy.

ELEMENTS OF A NEW MONETARY TECHNOLOGY

But this transformation did not come easily. The central banks could reestablish a firm hand over key domestic financial indicators only after they had learned to supplement, or to replace, the traditional policy instruments with new tools or novel adaptations of older ones.

[4] Ira O. Scott and Wilson E. Schmidt, "Imported Inflation and Monetary Policy," *Banca Nazionale del Lavoro Quarterly Review*, No. 71 (December 1964), p. 395. See also Peter M. Oppenheimer, "Imported Inflation and Monetary Policy: A Comment" and the rejoinder by Scott and Schmidt in *ibid.*, No. 73 (June 1965), pp. 191-200.

[5] Friedrich A. Lutz, "World Inflation and Domestic Monetary Stability," *ibid.*, p. 114.

[6] Quoted in Scott and Schmidt, *op.cit.*, pp. 3, 4.

Their willingness to experiment and to accept innovation was a recognition of the need to broaden the scope, and to speed up the effectiveness, of credit action. The authorities recognized that, because the dependence of domestic banks upon the central bank was much reduced after 1958, new ways had to be found to force them once again to seek central-bank accommodation or, alternatively, to limit directly their new credits. Partly because of continuing excess demand and tight labor markets in their economies, European central banks also sought to speed up the response of the banking system to monetary action: in particular, they wanted in a period of restraint to achieve a prompt slowdown in the rate of loan expansion. Finally, they often sought new policy instruments in order to achieve a more selective impact than could be achieved through general measures of restraint.

The additional policy tools which the European central banks developed make the period from 1958 to 1967 a creative chapter in the continuing evolution of the art of central banking. The process through which these new instruments emerged can best be understood against the background of the experience of the individual central bank. But an outline of the general character of the new technology may be a helpful introduction to the review of technical developments in each of the countries of the Common Market which will be presented in the following chapters.

Non-Price Credit Rationing

The characteristic which perhaps best distinguishes the new monetary technology from the orthodox tradition of central banking was an unprecedented emphasis upon credit rationing. The central banks were prepared to reduce the rate of new extensions of credit by preventing banks from lending, even in circumstances where they could not allow advances in domestic interest rates which would reduce the demand for funds. To limit availability, these central banks imposed quantitative limitations—both on their own credits to the commercial banks and on credits by commercial banks to the private sector.

At the central-bank level, much greater use was made of non-price measures to limit borrowings of the banking system, especially in Germany, France, and Belgium in the period under review.[7] In Ger-

---

[7] In Italy, rediscounting was not an important credit source until late in 1963 when the banks began to expand their central-bank borrowings. Since the discount rate was not changed in Italy between 1958 and 1967, it is evident that the mone-

5

many, announced reductions in rediscount quotas at the central bank were a particularly important measure of restraint after 1964. In Belgium and France, restraint took the form not of changes in the bank's rediscount quotas but of variations in the terms and conditions of discounting. Actions taken included changes in the administration of discount operations, in eligibility and acceptability requirements, in the prior authorization of trade credits by the central bank, and in the liquidity regulations which affected certain assets (such as medium-term paper in France) that the banks might otherwise present to the central bank.[8] The various non-price measures to ration central-bank credit in the countries in the European Economic Community were fully consistent with Garvy's conclusion that "the most significant" recent development in the field of discounting has been "resort to quantitative limitations, and thus diminished use of the (discount) rate."[9]

Changes in the terms and conditions of discounting to make borrowing more difficult were used to support, and on occasion to replace, a rise in the discount rate. Fears of provoking disequilibrating inflows of capital often caused the European central banks to hesitate to advance the discount rate. In addition, a tightening in the conditions of rediscounting—even when they were made public—did not have the same effects on financial markets, on business expectations, and on banking and credit costs as the announcement of a rise in the discount rate. In mid-1964, the German authorities raised reserve requirements "as a means of using monetary policy to contain inflationary pressures without Bank rate."[10] Earlier, during the 1963-64 effort at stabilization, the Bank of France raised the discount rate only once by ½ per cent and applied it chiefly to borrowing from the central bank; the rates on Treasury and export bills were unchanged and the costs of commercial-bank credit increased by only ¼ per cent.

---

tary policies of the Bank of Italy were related to credit availabilities rather than to changes in cost.

In the Netherlands, the banking system's buildup of short-term assets abroad severely limits their need to seek central-bank accommodation.

[8] A general review of the discount mechanism in leading countries since World War II may be found in George Garvy, "The Discount Mechanism in Leading Industrial Countries Since World War II" (Board of Governors of the Federal Reserve System, July 1968). Detailed studies of discounting operations in principal countries are to be found in Part II: Belgium, pp. 71-84; France, pp. 98-124; Germany, pp. 125-37; Italy, pp. 138-51; and the Netherlands, pp. 166-79.

[9] Ibid., p. 16.

[10] The Banker (London), Vol. 114 (August 1964), p. 528.

At the level of commercial-bank credit, rationing imposed by central banks took the form of ceilings on bank loans to the private sector. Such regulations were in effect in France in 1958 and again from 1963 to 1965 as one component of a broad stabilization program. In the Netherlands, they became perhaps the primary tool of credit restraint from 1960 to 1967, at first temporarily, and later on a more permanent basis. They were in effect in Belgium, on a voluntary basis, from January 1964 to July 1965 and again from April 1966 to June 1967. These ceilings usually set an annual or a monthly rate of increase and sometimes stipulated specific penalties on any excess credits. On occasion, the authorities might cut back the authorized rate of increase as a measure of additional restraint. Use of such ceilings has been discussed in Germany, but the Bundesbank has never been given authority to impose them; they have never been employed in Italy.

Adjusting Foreign Positions of Domestic Banks

Increased use of measures to induce the commercial banks to make marginal liquidity adjustments in their foreign, rather than in their domestic, positions[11] was a second major tool developed particularly in Germany and Italy. These central banks introduced foreign-currency swap transactions with commercial banks in 1958-59 as a temporary offset to the foreign and domestic liquidity effects of payments surpluses at that time. But, with experience, regulations to affect the banks' net foreign position were broadened and were gradually relied on to help control domestic liquidity in these two countries (which did not employ direct ceilings to limit commercial-bank loans). The regulations were chiefly intended: (a) in periods of payments surpluses, to shift excess domestic liquidity into foreign financial markets; and (b) in periods of credit restraint, to limit the extent domestic banks could obtain domestic-currency liquidity, either by borrowing or by liquidating foreign assets.

Arrangements to encourage liquidity adjustments in foreign centers developed differently in the two countries. In Germany, foreign-currency swaps to induce the commercial banks to export funds were activated during periods of payments surpluses; but, to ensure that the commercial banks retained their liquid assets abroad during periods of credit stringency, the Bundesbank subsequently used differential reserve requirements and "offset" privileges.

[11] The regulation of the commercial-banking system's foreign transactions to control domestic liquidity was separate from any balance-of-payments objectives of such measures.

7

In Italy, where the commercial banks and residents have acted both as substantial borrowers and lenders in the Euro-dollar market, the authorities would instruct the banks to attain a specific *net* position in foreign currencies with nonresidents,[12] and the commercial banks were permitted to choose whether to make their adjustments on the foreign-currency asset or liability side of their balance sheet. The terms of the directive would be changed at times when the banks were in a particularly vulnerable position. A severe credit stringency was created in 1963 merely by instructing the banks to borrow no more abroad; they were then forced to turn to the central bank to replace the internal liquidity they were losing because of the deficit in external payments. In addition, through swap facilities offered by the Italian Exchange Office, the Italian banks were encouraged to place money-market assets abroad, particularly until the end of 1965.

Reduced Importance of Uniform Reserve Requirements

A third major change in central-banking practice was the tendency for European central banks to depend less upon *uniform* reserve ratios and more upon *special* reserve requirements between 1958 and 1967. By the end of this period, uniform reserve ratios, both of the cash and the liquid-asset variety, were less widely used in these countries than they had been in 1958 (see Table 1).

As a tool of credit, cash-reserve requirements have never been as significant in the countries of the European Economic Community as in the United States and the United Kingdom, and the importance of these requirements declined between 1958 and 1967 (see Table 1). In 1963 they were withdrawn in the Netherlands; they were tried only briefly in Belgium during 1964. In Germany, changes in cash ratios were used aggressively during 1959-60 but less actively in the period of restraint from 1964 to 1966. In Italy, cash requirements contributed to the arrest of inflation in the late 1940s but were much less important during the 1960s. A cash ratio was introduced in France in 1967 for the first time; it coincided with a phasing out of the liquidity-reserve requirement and has not yet been deployed as an effective tool of restraint.

Because a number of European central banks turned to liquidity reserve requirements in the decade after World War II, the shift away

[12] From the late 1950s, the Bank of Italy encouraged the commercial banks to make foreign-currency credits to Italian importers and exporters to bring down the cost of credit in the country.

COUNTRIES OF THE EUROPEAN ECONOMIC COMMUNITY: SUMMARY OF RESERVE REQUIREMENTS AND OTHER CREDIT-CONTROL TECHNIQUES, 1958 AND 1967

	Belgium[1]		France[2]		Germany[3]		Italy[4]		Netherlands[5]	
	1958	1967	1958	1967	1958	1967	1958	1967	1958	1967
Primary Reserve										
Vault cash and balances with central bank	4%	none	none	4% demand[d] 2% time	R-6-13%[h] NR-10-30%	R-5%-13%[h] NR-10-30%[i]	25%[j]	10%	10%	none
Secondary Reserve										
Total Liquid Assets	46-61%[a]	—	25%[e]	none	none	none	—	12½%	none	none
Treasury paper		none		—	—	—	25%[j]	—	—	—
Commercial paper	—	—		16%[f]	—	—	—	—	—	—
Rediscount Ceilings	Formal	Formal	Formal	Formal	Formal	Formal	Infor-mal	Infor-mal	none	none
Ceilings on Bank Lending	none	Occasion-ally[b]	Occa-sion-ally[g]	Occa-sion-ally[g]	none	none	none	none	none	Fre-quently[k]
Encouraging Capital Outflows	none	none[c]	none	none	none	Frequently	none	Fre-quently	none	Fre-quently

[1] *Belgium.* [a]In January 1959 the cover ratio (*coéfficient de couverture*), consisting of a variety of government-guaranteed securities, ranged from 46% for regional and special banks to 56% for medium-sized and 61% for major banks. [b]Voluntary ceilings for individual banks were in effect from January 1964 to July 1965 and from April 1966 to June 1967. [c]In 1966, to reduce domestic liquidity, the National Bank sold on the "free" foreign-exchange market part of the proceeds of the government's foreign borrowing.

[2] *France.* [d]These requirements were announced on January 21, 1967, and they became fully effective on October 21. [e]In January 1959 French banks were required to hold in Treasury bills 25% of deposit liabilities. (In 1960 a new system of minimum reserve requirements—*coéfficient de trésorerie*—required the banks to hold any combination of cash, Treasury certificates, export paper, and medium-term commercial paper against their deposits.) [f]Medium-term paper rediscountable at the Bank of France. [g]In March 1963, ceilings on bank lending were imposed and removed on June 30, 1965. Such ceilings had also been imposed from February 1958 to February 1959.

[3] *Germany.* [h]R=deposits of residents; NR=deposits of nonresidents. The percentage varies with size of banking institution and its geographic location. [i]In February 1967, reserve requirements for nonresident deposits became the same as for resident deposits.

[4] *Italy.* [j]Italian banks were required to hold a 25% reserve in the form of either balances at the central bank (which earned the same rate of interest as did Treasury bills) or Treasury bills. [k]Monetary policy is now being carried out through ceilings on bank-credit expansion.

[5] *Netherlands.*

from these ratios during the 1960s is particularly striking. Belgium first introduced a liquid-asset requirement in 1946, Italy in 1947, France in 1948, and the Netherlands in 1954.[13] A changed attitude toward such ratios emerged during the 1950s as the monetary authorities came to recognize, with experience, that these were less a means to restrain bank lending than they were a way to force commercial banks to finance the Treasury more cheaply. By 1967 Belgium had abolished such requirements overnight, and Italy had reduced them. More important, in Italy and in France the compulsory proportion of Treasury securities was steadily reduced (see Table 1). This change was made possible by the lessened dependence of the Treasury on the banking system in these countries, a result which was, of course, an outgrowth of the rebuilding of flows of private savings and the structural improvements in European financial markets which enabled the Treasury to be financed outside the banking system. In this sense, the reduced significance of liquidity ratios in European central banking can serve as one measure of the extent of financial rehabilitation that was realized in Italy, Belgium, and France between 1958 and 1967.

[13] Peter G. Fousek, *Foreign Central Banking: The Instruments of Monetary Policy* (Federal Reserve Bank of New York, 1957), pp. 57-68. The liquidity ratio in the Netherlands was on a stand-by basis only and has never been put into effect.

II. REVIEW OF EXPERIENCES IN INDIVIDUAL COUNTRIES

Against the background of these broad developments, there were important differences in the ways the individual European central banks chose to make credit policy effective in their own situation. Historical, institutional, and legal factors were bound to produce significant differences in approach from country to country. In addition, there were differences in the particular economic and political problems each of these countries faced, even though all of them participated in the general atmosphere of business buoyancy and external-payments strength which characterized the countries of the European Economic Community as a group during this period. The review of developments in each of these countries—Germany, Italy, France, the Netherlands, and Belgium—reveals that striking national differences in the use of the instruments of credit policy continue to be evident, despite the growing economic integration among the countries of the European Economic Community since 1958.

GERMANY: "EURO-DOLLAR OPERATIONS" AND REDISCOUNT QUOTAS

The first attempts of the German authorities to neutralize the domestic-credit effects of the large payments surpluses ended in failure. Between August 1959 and July 1960, cash reserve ratios were raised five times, the discount rate was increased three times, and the public authorities added to their balances at the central bank. As a result, the authorities were able to keep reserve accruals of DM 8 billion during 1960 from expanding the credit base by no more than DM 1.7 billion.[14] Despite the reserve accruals, in fact, credit institutions had to borrow DM 800 million to meet their liquidity needs.

But the German authorities discovered that their efforts were "in truth a labour of Sisyphus. On the one hand liquidity was drawn off, but on the other hand still more constantly flowed into the banks, even though in the second half of 1960 the cash transactions of the major public authorities also took large amounts of money away from them. . . . On the whole the object of the credit restrictions was thus not attained."[15] As a result, they "found that . . . the boom cannot be

---

[14] The Bundesbank estimated that higher reserve requirements absorbed DM 4 billion, increased public deposits at the central bank DM 2 billion, and increased security purchases by commercial banks DM 1.3 billion during 1960.

[15] Deutsche Bundesbank, *Annual Report*, 1960, p. 5.

11

brought under control by means of credit policy alone, particularly since the pressure . . . on internal liquidity was increasingly offset through the taking in of foreign money. . . . To ward off this very large exchange inflow, the Bundesbank was obliged from November onwards to lower the German interest rate level."[16]

Reductions in the discount rate in November 1960 and again in January 1961 could not resolve this conflict between domestic and external objectives. The easing of credit—to make credit restraint more effective—ran into opposition because German officials outside the central bank were prepared to agree "to the discount rate reductions . . . but intimated objection . . . to lower minimum reserve ratios as well . . . in the light of the recent . . . upturn of the business cycle."[17]

The continued capital inflows and the unwillingness of economic officials to sanction further easing of domestic credit culminated in the decision to revalue the DM by 5 per cent in March. The authorities had considered, as an alternative, "negative exchange control" to isolate German financial markets, but such action would "simply not accord with the present degree of convertibility of currencies."[18] Revaluation of the DM followed.

Foreign-Currency Swaps with Commercial Banks

After this experience, the German authorities did not again use reserve requirements so aggressively to absorb excess liquidity from abroad. Instead, to offset incoming liquidity during periods of payments surplus, they developed "open-market operations in the Euro-dollar market."

This approach had its beginning in the undertaking of the Bundesbank early in 1959 to provide the commercial banks spot dollars with exchange cover back into DMs. By mid-1959, however, only about one-third of holdings by commercial banks were covered by these swaps because the rates were not particularly attractive to them.

After mid-1960, when interest rates advanced sharply in Germany and turned downward in the United States, the banks accelerated the repatriation of their foreign assets. The Bundesbank halted and reversed this repatriation by offering a large premium on the forward dollar, and by June 1961 outstanding swap contracts exceeded DM 3 billion (see Table 2). These contracts began to be run off late in 1961, although a few were still outstanding by the end of 1962.

[16] Deutsche Bundesbank, *Monthly Report*, March 1961, p. 4.
[17] *Loc.cit.*   [18] *Loc.cit.*

TABLE 2

GERMAN COMMERCIAL BANKS: FOREIGN MONEY-MARKET ASSETS AND
SWAP COMMITMENTS WITH BUNDESBANK, SELECTED DATES 1959 TO 1968
(in millions of DM)

		Swap contracts with Bundesbank	Not covered by Bundesbank swaps	Total foreign money-market assets
1958:	December	—	1.0	1.0
1959:	June	1.0	1.7	2.7
	December	0.7	1.8	2.5
1960:	June	0.2	1.0	1.2
	December	0.4	0.9	1.3
1961:	June	3.1	1.7	4.8
	December	1.1	1.7	2.8
1962:	June	2.2	1.9	4.1
	December	0.2	2.3	2.5
1963:	June	—	3.6	3.6
	December	—	2.8	2.8
1964:	December	0.4	2.9	3.3
1965:	December	—	3.6	3.6
1966:	December	—	3.5	3.5
1967:	June	—	6.8	6.8
	December	2.5	5.0	7.5
1968:	March	3.4	5.5	8.9

SOURCES: 1958 to June 1963, Ekhard Brehmer, "Official Forward Exchange Operations: The German Experience," International Monetary Fund *Staff Papers*, Vol. XI (November 1964), p. 394. December 1963 to March 1968, Deutsche Bundesbank *Monthly Report*.

Large Trade Surplus Again in Late 1963

The emergence of a sizable trade surplus after mid-1963, in large part a result of inflationary developments in France and Italy, induced the authorities to tighten the "passive"[19] credit policy, which had been appropriate for the period of weaker internal demand in late 1961 and 1962. By April 1964 the authorities had to act to reduce the net capital inflows. To stimulate outflows, the banks were offered forward-dollar swaps at above-market rates provided the funds were invested in U.S. Treasury bills (that is, not in the Euro-dollar market). To reduce inflows, a proposal was made to impose a withholding tax of 25 per cent on nonresident holdings of German domestic bonds. Even though the proposal did not become law until February 1965, it had an immediate effect on the capital market, stimulating substantial sales

[19] That is, the authorities allowed operating factors—the growth in credit and in the note circulation—gradually to tighten bank liquidity.

13

of German securities by foreigners. In addition, the withdrawal of a 2 per cent tax on new issues, and the exemption from the withholding tax of nonresident DM bonds placed with nonresidents, produced sizable foreign flotations in Germany in 1964.

These measures, together with effective stabilization actions in Italy and France which slowed the expansion in German exports, averted what had threatened to be a disequilibrating payments surplus of major proportions. Fortunately, monetary conditions had tightened abroad and interest rates had been rising since 1964 in most other developed countries. As a result, the Bundesbank was able to raise reserve requirements by 10 per cent in August 1964 and the discount rate in January—without provoking unmanageable inflows of capital.

The cumulative effects of these measures had begun to check the rate of growth in bank credit and in capital spending by mid-1965, but the strength of the business expansion required a further tightening of the credit situation. Continued advances in foreign interest rates, and control measures taken by the United States and Britain to reduce outflows of capital helped to reduce the inflows of foreign funds in the face of growing domestic stringency. Moreover, a substantial deficit appeared in the German current account by the second quarter of 1965, the first since 1951 (see Table 6 below).

In this environment, additional credit measures were introduced. The discount rate was raised from 3½ to 4 per cent in August 1965 and to 5 per cent in May 1966. The rediscount quotas for all credit institutions were reduced in October 1965 and again in May 1966, and selling rates on open-market paper were advanced several times.

By early 1966, this extended period of credit restraint produced a severe domestic credit stringency. The banks were forced to borrow heavily from the Bundesbank (see Table 3), and major strains developed in the German capital market. A moratorium on public-sector flotations was agreed in the spring. But bond yields continued to climb, reaching a peak in the third quarter: in August 1966 new issues averaged a high of 8.6 per cent, outstanding issues 8.1 per cent.

Recession and Trade Surplus

This protracted period of domestic restraint corrected the external deficit. By the third quarter of 1966, the current account was again in small surplus; by the fourth quarter, the trade surplus was approaching record levels, largely because imports had stabilized and exports had expanded sharply (see Table 6 below). In 1967 the foreign-trade

14

TABLE 3

GERMANY: PRINCIPAL CHANGES IN BANK LIQUIDITY AND COMMERCIAL-BANK LIQUID ASSETS, 1962 TO 1967
(in billions of DM)

Period	Reductions of bank liquidity taking form of:				Distribution of banks' liquid assets: (end of period)		
	Sales of open-market paper	Sales of liquid assets abroad	Borrowings from Bundesbank	Total uses of liquidity	Domestic-asset holdings	Foreign-asset holdings	Total assets
1962	.7	— .1	.5	1.1	4.9	2.2	7.1
1963	— .7	— .4	— .2	—1.2	5.9	2.5	8.4
1964	2.2	— .9	2.0	3.3ᵃ	4.0	3.3	7.3
1965	1.9	.2	1.6	3.7	3.0	3.6	6.8
1966	.4	— .9	.8	.2ᵇ	3.9	3.5	7.4
1967	—2.1	—3.5	—1.6	—7.2	10.3	7.5	17.8

ᵃ For comparison purposes, the increase of 10 per cent in required reserves in August 1964 (not included in this table) absorbed about DM 1.1 billion in reserve balances.

ᵇ Similarly, the increase of 10 per cent in required reserves in January 1966 absorbed about DM 1.2 billion in reserve balances.

SOURCE: Deutsche Bundesbank *Monthly Report*, Table 1 "Overall Monetary Survey," "2. Bank Liquidity." Data not available in this form before 1962.

surplus reached the unprecedented level of DM 16.9 billion for the year.

On the domestic side, the German economy entered its most serious postwar recession after mid-1966. By the third quarter, investment and credit demands both had slumped appreciably, accompanied by a slowdown in home investment in manufacturing and by a reduced level of capacity utilization.

Aggressive Monetary Ease

The extended decline in economic activity led the authorities by late 1966 to adopt a policy of active ease and to introduce two special programs of public-sector investment to spur business recovery.[20] On the monetary front, required reserves were reduced six times, and the discount rate five times, between December 1966 and September 1967. The sluggish demand for domestic credit meant that much of the added liquidity was placed in the Euro-dollar market by the German banks.

By November 1967 the continuing trade surplus induced the authorities to reintroduce swap facilities to encourage the banks to place funds abroad to ease the international impact of Germany's payments surpluses. By March 1968 these contracts amounted to almost DM 3.4 billion, and the foreign assets of the banks had accumulated to an unprecedented DM 8.9 billion (see Table 2).

Crucial Role of "Swaps" in German Credit Policy

The swap arrangements in Germany took the form of purchases of forward dollars by the Bundesbank from the large commercial banks at rates established, and varied, by the central bank. The rates bore no necessary relationship to the cost of forward cover for commercial transactions in the foreign-exchange market; they were, instead, related to differentials between German and foreign money rates and were changed as the central bank sought to speed up—and to slow down—the placement of banking funds abroad.

Because the banks were placing abroad only funds surplus to their domestic requirements, the swaps have sometimes been considered to be of subsidiary significance. Because the assets remained available to the German banks, it has not always been clear that the swaps really reduced domestic liquidity to any significant extent.

[20] See "Economic Upswing in Western Europe," *Federal Reserve Bulletin* (November 1968), pp. 883-899.

Evaluations of this character do not do justice to the contribution that the swap operations made to the internal effectiveness of credit measures in Germany during periods of current-account surplus and domestic boom, such as occurred in 1960-61 and again in 1964. The swaps, a form of "open-market operations" in foreign-money markets, neutralized the primary (and thereby avoided the secondary) effects of external-payments surpluses on domestic liquidity. Without neutralization, banks with additional liquidity from abroad would have increased their loans and placed excess funds in the German interbank loan market. In that case, German credit institutions—both large and small—which could borrow in the internal (but not in foreign) financial markets, would have been able to postpone borrowing from the central bank. To that extent, the effectiveness of the rediscount quotas —a primary instrument for controlling bank lending in 1965 and 1966[21]—would have been seriously reduced.

Measures to Check Repatriations

But there was always the danger that the banks would respond to periods of internal credit restraint by repatriating their foreign assets, as they had in 1959 and 1960. Between September 1959 and March 1960, just after the swap arrangements had been introduced, the Bundesbank estimated that nearly one-third of its foreign-exchange accruals consisted of funds repatriated by the banks.[22]

During 1961, the Bundesbank checked this repatriation by making the swap premium more attractive as interest-rate differentials changed. Thereafter, they chose another approach to attain the same objective: the use of special reserve requirements on nonresident deposits. Reserve requirements on these deposits were raised above those for resident deposits,[23] and the banks were permitted to use money-market assets held abroad to meet these requirements. Through the "compensation privilege" or "offset right," as this facility was known, the central bank added substantially—at times as much as 1 per cent per annum— to the effective yield on money-market assets in foreign centers.

[21] Until 1964 the German credit institutions had made only limited use of their rediscount facilities at the central bank. But the tightening of bank liquidity in Germany in 1965 and 1966 led to a rapid expansion in discounting. At their peak in May 1966, rediscounts were, in the aggregate, more than 50 per cent of the authorized quotas for the banking system.

[22] Deutsche Bundesbank *Annual Report*, 1959, p. 37.

[23] Differential (higher) reserve ratios on nonresident liabilities were in effect from May 1957 to March 1959, from January 1960 to January 1962, and from March 1964 to February 1967.

During the protracted credit restraint from 1964 to 1966, this approach effectively discouraged repatriations. Even though liquidity pressures mounted and required reserves were increased in August 1964 and again in January 1966, the banking system as a whole sold domestic open-market paper and borrowed from the central bank; the banks did not reduce their short-term foreign assets significantly. In 1964 the banks sold DM 2.2 billion of German open-market paper and borrowed DM 2 billion from the central bank, but also added slightly to their foreign assets (see Table 3). In 1965 they repatriated only DM 150 million from abroad but sold DM 1.9 billion of open-market paper and borrowed DM 1.6 billion from the central bank.

The German banks could obtain liquidity from abroad by borrowing as well as by repatriating their own assets. To discourage this, liabilities to nonresidents in foreign currencies were made subject to reserve requirements, and short-term credits from banks abroad were treated, in computing required reserves, as time deposits. Then on August 1, 1964, the rediscount quota of each credit institution was reduced by the amount of any borrowing abroad—that is, by any increase in gross liabilities in excess of the January-June 1964 average. German banks had earlier been forbidden to pay interest on nonresident deposits.

The transformation of the German domestic and external position after mid-1966 led the Bundesbank to alter its foreign-currency regulations. The offset rights of the German banks were eliminated at the beginning of 1967, after German interest rates had declined substantially below those in foreign centers. Then in November 1967, large-scale inflows of private capital into Germany during the sterling-devaluation crisis induced the central bank to reintroduce swap facilities. The swaps were again placed on offer in March 1968 when speculation in the gold market produced a new inflow of private funds into Germany, and some DM 3.4 billion were outstanding in March (see Table 2).

ITALY: MANAGING THE BANKS' NET FOREIGN POSITION

Actions to affect the foreign-currency positions of the banks were the major tools used by the Italian authorities in constraining the commercial banks to make domestic credit adjustments. They continuously maintained quantitative limits on the *net* foreign positions of the banks. When they wished to bring about domestic credit adjustments, they proceeded to change the directives. They were particularly successful in tightening internal credit conditions by limiting inflows, thus producing a severe credit stringency during the balance-of-payments crisis in mid-1963 (the only period of substantial restraint in Italy between 1958 and 1967) merely by prohibiting further commercial bank borrowings abroad.

The Introduction of Foreign-Currency Swaps

In November 1959, with the external accounts in substantial surplus, forward-exchange swaps were introduced in Italy, chiefly to encourage the banks to maintain or expand their low-rate loans to domestic customers in foreign currencies. Late in 1960 the swaps also helped to reduce internal liquidity during a period of substantial surplus. Under this arrangement, the commercial banks were permitted to buy spot dollars (at the market rate of exchange) from the Italian Exchange Office and to resell them at the same time at the same rate. This facility was quite advantageous for the banks. Had they tried to obtain forward cover in the foreign-exchange market, a substantial premium would undoubtedly have emerged on the forward lira against the dollar, and foreign placements would have ceased to be profitable.

The Italian banks took advantage of this offer on a substantial scale —enough, in fact, to enable them to cover the large volume of liabilities to foreigners that they had built up in the 1950s. When the Bank of Italy, in August 1960, instructed the Italian banks to pay off all *net* liabilities to foreigners which were denominated in foreign currencies, they mostly acquired dollars from the Exchange Office and placed them in the rapidly expanding Euro-dollar market. By January 1961 they had in fact complied with the terms of the central bank's directive.

But the emphasis of economic policy altered in Italy during 1961 and 1962, and with it the objectives of monetary policy changed. The endeavor to stimulate rapid economic growth brought an active government-spending program and a willingness of Italian entrepreneurs to grant wage increases substantially in excess of the growth in productivity.

Monetary policy eased. Instead of trying to sterilize excess liquidity from abroad, the Bank of Italy took steps to ease the liquidity position of credit institutions, especially as the external surplus declined during the course of 1962. In January 1962 minimum reserve requirements were cut, and in November the proscription against any net foreign liabilities in foreign currencies was removed.

Several considerations contributed to the ease in credit policy at this time. With incomes rising rapidly, the authorities feared that greater credit restraint would merely have reduced investment, thereby permitting consumption to claim a larger share of aggregate resources, the opposite of official priorities. Further, they feared that tighter credit would have added to the payments surplus, at least during 1961.

In addition, the authorities were thinking in terms of a longer-run reformation in Italy's financial structure and its level of interest rates. Late in 1962 they introduced a broad program of reform to create a flexible money market, to broaden the capital market, and to integrate Italian financial markets more closely into those abroad. The monetary objectives of this program included:

(a) To shift loanable funds, previously absorbed by the Treasury, to the private sector,
(b) To convert short-term into longer-term credits,
(c) To bring about a general decline in all interest rates.

This program comprised several elements. To create a money market, Treasury bills were to be issued by monthly tender, and the rates on interbank deposits were held to the current yield on Treasury bills (so that small banks would shift into productive loans and risk assets). To integrate domestic and foreign financial markets, in November 1962 the Bank of Italy withdrew the directive that each bank should balance its net position. The banks responded by borrowing heavily in the Euro-dollar market.

Foreign Borrowings and the Foreign-Exchange Crisis of 1963

The government's vigorous growth policy, accompanied by the monetary easing, was the prelude to a period of accelerated internal inflation in Italy, marked by a burst of wage increases that—reinforced by domestic political uncertainties which stimulated outflows of capital and delayed decisive governmental action to strengthen the current account—produced a major foreign-exchange crisis in late 1963. The banks borrowed heavily abroad—some $1.2 billion in the ten months from October 1962 to the end of August 1963—to meet the soaring loan demands associated with internal inflationary conditions. These borrowings provided the banks with the additional internal liquidity they required and also had the effect of obscuring the magnitude of the deterioration of Italy's external position in late 1962 and 1963. Because of the sensitive Italian political situation, the government was at that particular time especially anxious to avoid a decline in the official reserves equivalent to the deteriorating balance-of-payments situation.

The large, and by late 1963 critical, extent of the balance-of-payments deterioration forced the authorities to act. They moved first on the credit side and only later, after the coalition had reestablished a working government, did they act on the fiscal front by raising several consumer taxes and by seeking in early 1964 to decelerate the growth in local-government spending.

The key measure of credit restraint, which produced rapid and dramatic results on the payments position, was a directive in September 1963 that the banks were to hold their net foreign liabilities to the level of August 31. This instruction meant that the banks could no longer obtain domestic liquidity through borrowings abroad and had to watch the large balance-of-payments deficit contract their domestic cash base. They could obtain relief only from the Bank of Italy. So effective was this crunch that the central bank actually acquired substantial lira assets to cushion this process of contraction.

From this experience the authorities decided not to allow the commercial banks to borrow abroad again on a comparable scale. The banks gradually reduced their net foreign liabilities. The recession in domestic activity in Italy, which was produced by the attempts at stabilization in 1963, led to a shift in credit policy from severe restraint to one of ease during the course of 1964. By late 1964 the balance of payments had again returned to large surplus. With Italian credit demands still sluggish, the banks built up their foreign assets (see Table 4). Between the end of 1964 and 1965, their foreign-currency

TABLE 4

ITALIAN COMMERCIAL BANKS: FOREIGN-CURRENCY POSITION WITH FOREIGN RESIDENTS, 1958 TO 1967

End of Period	In millions of dollars equivalent		
	Assets	Liabilities	Net Position
1958	252	535	—273
1959	416	696	—280
1960	707	710	— 3
1961	932	877	65
1962	1,384	1,741	—363
1963	1,190	2,165	—965
1964	1,309	1,943	—634
1965	2,312	2,210	102
1966	3,093	2,590	503
1967	3,370	3,002	368

SOURCE: Bank of Italy *Bulletin* (Bimonthly), Table 71.

swap contracts with the Exchange Office had increased from $320 million to $1,531 million. By September 1965 they had shifted to a net foreign-asset position for the first time since October 1962.

At the end of 1965 the authorities then instructed the banks that any bank with a net asset position would not be allowed in the future to revert to a net liability position. This directive, designed to strengthen the authorities' control over bank liquidity, proved to be effective when, during the renewed expansion in Italy in 1967, the banks began to decrease some of their net foreign assets. Because of this limitation, they could not carry this process very far.

At the same time, the authorities also withdrew the right of banks with net assets abroad to obtain preferential forward-exchange facilities at the Exchange Office. These banks could sell forward dollars only at a discount (premium on the forward lira) prevailing in the commercial market. Only banks with a net liability position abroad could continue to obtain additional swaps at a flat rate, equal to the spot rate for the dollar in the market. (They could still renew outstanding swaps at maturity.) This directive was designed to encourage the banks with net foreign-asset positions to step up their lira loans and security purchases, thereby helping to bring down Italian interest rates.

FRANCE: CEILINGS ON BANK LOANS
AND ADJUSTMENTS OF DOMESTIC LIQUIDITY

During the period under review, the French authorities found it necessary to undertake comprehensive stabilization plans to defend the parity of the currency, once in 1957-58 when the franc was formally stabilized at a devalued parity, and again in September 1963, when inflationary developments had gathered momentum and the current account had shifted into deficit. On both these occasions the government introduced a broad program of restraint which included, in addition to direct controls on bank loans to the private sector, substantial measures in the areas of taxes and spending, in debt-management operations, and in the use of price controls. Credit policy was less important in the French efforts at stabilization than it had been in the German and the Italian.

The Bank of France was bound to find it difficult to bring the liquidity positions of the banking system under control because of the magnitude of official reserve accruals. Between 1960 and 1966 these reserve gains accounted for nearly 80 per cent of the expansion of the cash base of the banking system. In this situation, the authorities had to devise measures to limit bank liquidity, and they relied largely on the administration of the discount window of the Bank of France and on liquid-asset reserve requirements. In addition, the curtailment of inflows of foreign funds was to become an objective of credit policy. The Bank of France chose to discourage inflows of capital, not by measures to regulate the foreign positions of the French banks, as in Germany and Italy, but by making domestic credit adjustments to discourage such inward movements: they held down the money rates in the Paris market to avoid the emergence of incentives to import funds.

The French preference to have the banks make their liquidity adjustments in domestic, and not in foreign, financial markets can in part be attributed to a tendency on the part of the authorities to regard short-term flows of capital between France and the outside world with suspicion, if not as a potential source of disturbance. For this reason, French banks were required to keep a balanced overall position in each foreign currency from 1958 until the regulations were altered at the end of 1966.[24] This directive was designed to insulate the banking system from international developments and particularly to try to limit inward or outward flows of short-term funds.

Two other considerations conditioned the policy of limiting the operations of French banks between francs and foreign currencies. The French authorities viewed the continuing accruals of official reserves not as a disturbance to be offset or eliminated but as a symbol of economic (and political) stability and financial strength. They also recognized no international considerations that made it desirable to disguise official reserve gains. Furthermore, the authorities sought to achieve a major reconstruction of the French financial markets and the banking system, and growing reserves contributed to domestic confidence.

Stabilization Program in 1957-58

The French government introduced a wide range of restrictive measures to ensure that the 1957-58 devaluation of the franc would be successful: the discount rate was raised in two steps from 3 to 5 per cent, rediscount ceilings were cut back three times between July and November 1957, the Bank of France was no longer required by

[24] The details of the rather complex French regulations governing the operations of their commercial banks are found in Rodney H. Mills, "The Regulation of Short-Term Capital Movements: Western European Techniques in the 1960's," Staff Economic Studies No. 46, Federal Reserve Board, May 22, 1968, esp. pp. 30-32.

law to rediscount Treasury bills held by the banks in excess of their liquid-asset ratios, and a ceiling was placed on bank lending. In addition, regulations on installment credit were tightened, as were credits to the nationalized industries and for housing. A medium-term financing institution was also established to provide an alternative source for refinancing such credits in lieu of the central bank.

A major improvement in the Treasury's finances supported the credit restraints. The previously large deficit was almost eliminated. A highly successful gold-clause loan issued in mid-1958 enabled the Treasury to obtain substantial financing outside the banking system. By early 1959, in fact, the credit position was relaxed: the ceilings on short- and medium-term bank credit were removed and the discount rate reduced.

The improved external position—from better export earnings, stabilized imports, repatriation of funds from abroad, and an inflow of new capital—coincided with a new interest on the part of French residents to acquire financial assets, and there was a notable easing in credit-market conditions. Even when domestic investment demand rose sharply in 1960, particularly for inventories, and the demand for bank credit picked up, there was a comparable growth in domestic savings moving into financial instruments.

The growth in private savings and in the Treasury's surplus were major reasons that the authorities did not take steps to restrain domestic liquidity in 1960. The Treasury had net savings (on a national-accounts basis) in 1959 and 1960, and was able to borrow funds outside the banks for the various lending programs and for debt repayment. In this environment, interest rates continued to decline. At the same time, domestic liquidity was reduced by Treasury repayments of foreign and intercentral-bank indebtedness.

At the end of 1960 the situation had improved sufficiently for the authorities to introduce a new system of liquidity requirements, which began to free the banks from being *required* to hold Treasury paper but which did require them to hold medium-term private paper (see Table 1). Formerly, French banks had to hold 25 per cent of deposits in Treasury bills. Under the new arrangement, a liquid-asset ratio of 30 per cent was set, but only 20 per cent was to be in Treasury bills. The overall reserve ratio was raised later (as part of the 1963 program of stabilization), but the Treasury-bill component was steadily reduced: it was down to 10 per cent by mid-1964 and was entirely eliminated at the end of 1966.

Stabilization Measures in 1963

In the course of 1962 and 1963, inflationary symptoms became more widespread, and monetary policy became somewhat more restrictive. But the degree of restraint was limited. In these years a number of measures to improve the structure of financial markets in France, similar to those introduced at that time in Italy, including the establishment of a system of Treasury-bill tender, were put into effect.

But the intensification of inflationary pressures prompted the authorities to announce a comprehensive stabilization program. The ceiling on the growth in bank credit, which had been restored in February, was cut back; the discount rate was raised by ½ per cent for borrowings from the central bank but by only ¼ per cent on bank credits; installment-credit terms tightened; the Treasury issued additional long-term loans to sop up liquidity in September 1963 and again in March 1964; French banks were prohibited from paying interest on non-resident franc accounts; and stricter terms were imposed on borrowings by franc-area residents. Controls were also imposed on industrial prices. Emphasis was put on the need for an income policy for the public-sector employees, and the budget estimates for 1965, as announced in September 1964, projected an elimination of the deficit.

During 1964 the current-account deterioration came to an end (see Table 6). But credit policy remained restrictive; the rate of expansion of bank credit was limited to only 9 per cent in 1964 compared to 18 per cent in 1962 and 14 per cent in 1963.

By mid-1965 a slowdown in business expansion had become apparent and the current account had strengthened. With budget policy restraining demand and helping to increase savings, the Bank of France moved to relax credit policy. In April the discount rate was returned to the prestabilization level of 3½ per cent and in June the ceilings on bank loans were removed.

At this time, the government authorized the private banks to compete for deposits and savings with the public financial institutions as an added structural reform designed to increase competition and to improve French financial markets.

Two additional banking reforms were introduced in 1967; they can be regarded as symbols of the major financial reformation that the authorities had been able to achieve since 1958. In the first place, the withdrawal of the compulsory liquid-asset ratio was begun in January

1967 with the introduction of a cash (non-interest-earning) reserve at the Bank of France. For the first time in recent French history, the banks were no longer *required* to hold any Treasury obligations against their deposit liabilities. Shortly thereafter, virtually full capital-account convertibility was achieved.

NETHERLANDS: LOAN CEILINGS AND "PENALTY RESERVES"

The central instrument of credit restraint in the Netherlands has been ceilings on bank lending to the private sector, combined with "penalty" cash deposits on any excess credits. Prior to the wage explosion late in 1963, the commercial banks also built up their money-market assets abroad, a movement stimulated by the relatively low level of Dutch rates compared to those abroad. Because of the banks' large foreign assets, much of the adjustment of their domestic liquidity takes place through changes in those assets. The Netherlands Bank also decided to withdraw the cash reserve ratio as a policy tool because, in the words of the Bank, "the resulting sterilization of liquidity would have led to sales of foreign exchange . . . without effectively reducing the liquidity of the banks."[25] The sharp rise in Netherlands interest rates when credit policy was tightened in 1964-65 slowed down further foreign-currency accruals by the banks. The government also used debt-measurement operations to absorb domestic liquidity, in support of credit policy, especially from 1959 to 1961.

Reserve Requirements and Treasury Debt Operations

To neutralize the payments surpluses after 1958, the authorities raised reserve requirements from 4 to 10 per cent and absorbed liquidity through debt operations. The Treasury improved its cash position and also repaid indebtedness to the banking system through additional market borrowings.

The debt operations were continued into 1959 when another external surplus was achieved. Short-term Treasury paper was bought from the banks to keep Dutch short rates below those abroad; in this way, the banks had a strong incentive to place excess liquid funds abroad. With their foreign assets at such a high level, the central bank feared that the banks would repatriate them if credit was tightened. For this reason, the banks were warned in the spring of 1960 that a ceiling on loans would be imposed—if there was to be an undue credit expansion —and they would be required to place interest-free deposits at the

[25] Netherlands Bank, *Annual Report*, 1964, p. 104.

26

central bank to offset any excess lending. This "penalty" reserve deposit was intended to ensure that, if the banks attempted to meet the needs of credit-worthy customers outside the quotas, they would do so only at a loss.

During 1960 the government had to proceed more vigorously than in 1959 to offset the foreign-exchange purchases of the central bank because a more rapid decline in interest rates abroad than in the Netherlands reduced the incentive for the banks to place funds abroad. The country's foreign-currency assets rose by FL 1,660 million, of which only FL 240 million were acquired by the Dutch banks. Public-sector operations sterilized these accumulations. The Treasury used a surplus of FL 440 million revenue and some FL 630 million of capital-market borrowings to improve its balance at the central bank. In addition, some FL 400 million raised in the capital market was employed to reduce outstanding floating debt. The magnitude of these public-sector fiscal and debt operations can be seen by the fact that a 1 per cent rise in reserve requirements absorbed only FL 80 million of liquidity.

The First Use of Credit Ceilings

With the revaluation of the guilder by 5 per cent in March 1961, the reduced external payments surplus ceased to be an important liquidity-generating factor. But domestic credit was expanding rapidly, and the authorities introduced the ceiling on loans and the penalty-deposit system in July. A monthly rate of increase of 1 per cent was permitted during 1961 and one of ½ per cent during the first few months of 1962. The authorities also intervened to keep money-market rates low enough to stimulate short-term placements abroad, both to check official foreign-exchange accruals and to limit domestic expansion. But the cost of forward cover (the discount on the forward dollar) during much of the year encouraged the banks to repatriate funds from abroad.

An easing of inflationary impulses, both domestic and from abroad, diminished sufficiently for the authorities to suspend the credit ceilings at the end of 1962. But they had to be reactivated in September 1963 and renewed regularly until 1967. A delayed wage-price push associated with the state of overfull demand, especially in the labor market, built up rapidly during 1963 and culminated in a "wage explosion"— that is, bargaining contracts concluded in the autumn of 1963 produced wage increases of around 15 per cent during 1964.

Clearly a major stabilization effort had become necessary. Tax and spending actions were taken on the fiscal front and, on the monetary, ceilings were imposed. When the monthly rate of increase of 1 per cent was exceeded in late 1963 and early 1964, the banks were required to make "penalty" deposits. The authorities again used public-sector financing operations to offset the Netherlands Bank's net acquisition of some FL 600 million of foreign currencies. The growth in note circulation and new loan extensions strained the liquidity positions of the banks. By stages, the central bank reduced required reserves from the 5 per cent level and eliminated them entirely at the end of 1963. Since then, uniform reserve requirements have not been reimposed.

Credit Restraint and the End of an Era of Cheap Money

The sharp rise in imports forced the banks to draw on their foreign assets to restore their domestic liquidity. During 1964 and 1965 public-sector spending was expansionary, and credit policy had to assume the burden of domestic stabilization. The authorities used a range of policy tools. Loan ceilings were lowered in mid-1965 and, after they were exceeded in early 1966, were reduced again in mid-1966. The discount rate was raised from 4½ to 5 per cent in May 1966.

The authorities also decided at this time to abandon their extended efforts to keep interest rates in the Netherlands below those in neighboring countries of the European Economic Community. Yields on government bonds climbed above 6½ per cent and those on industrial bonds above 7½ per cent. Back in mid-1963 the yield on long government bonds had been only 4.31 per cent.

BELGIUM: LOAN CEILINGS AND DISCOUNT ADMINISTRATION

Between 1958 and 1967 the Belgian authorities faced the problem of coping with strong external influences on bank liquidity. The country's vulnerability to foreign influences (a result of the dependence on foreign trade and the increased capital mobility of the period) was to tax the arsenal of policy tools which the central bank could use. The authorities employed a variety of tools—particularly adjustments in discounting costs and availabilities, Treasury borrowings abroad, and voluntary credit ceilings—in their attempts to make credit restraint effective.[26] Since 1964 the ceiling on bank loans and changes in the

[26] For details, see George Garvy, "The Discount Mechanism in Leading Industrial Countries Since World War II," Board of Governors of the Federal Reserve System (July 1968), pp. 74ff.

cost and availability of discount facilities have probably been the principal policy instruments. During this period, the authorities also carried out a major reformation of the country's financial structure by seeking to improve the functioning of financial markets and to attain a lower level of interest rates to spur industrial modernization and expansion.

Belgian Economy Sluggish in 1958

The protracted decline in business activity during the Europe-wide recession in 1958 produced in Belgium relatively easy borrowing conditions in the capital market, and the central bank encouraged a further easing in domestic interest rates. Because the Treasury's financing requirements dominated domestic markets, the private economy was not able to take full advantage of this period of relative ease. Then, at the end of 1959, the discount rate was raised from 3¼ to 4 per cent, but the purpose was not to reduce bank lending but to discourage the banks' placements of short-term assets abroad.

The Congo crisis in mid-1960 produced serious external strains, and the authorities promptly took defensive measures. The discount rate was raised from 4 to 5 per cent, and the yield on five- to thirty-year Treasury bonds rose from 5.21 per cent at the end of 1959 to 6.07 per cent a year later. By September 1960, however, the worst of these difficulties had been ridden out. Private outflows of capital began to be reversed, and official reserve holdings were replenished by substantial short-term borrowings abroad by the Treasury.

Reorganizing Belgian Industry and Finance

Once the independence of the Congo had become an established fact, the government began to plan ahead to enable Belgian industry to compete within the Common Market. The need to expand private investment and to accelerate industrial growth meant, for monetary policy, the attainment of lower levels of rates and more ample capital funds in domestic markets.

The main obstacle to further progress in this area was the Treasury's fiscal position since the Treasury's deficits were absorbing long-term funds. At the same time, the banks had liquidity from their excess holdings of government securities. The budgetary position eased during 1961, not only because of a marked reduction in the deficit but because the banks were encouraged (with forward cover provided by the central bank) to borrow abroad to finance holdings of short-term debt of the Treasury and of public institutions. The improved external payments position (and the finance of Treasury needs from abroad) permitted the central bank to reduce the discount rate gradually, from 4¼ per cent to 3½ per cent in the course of 1962. Yields on government bonds fell below 5½ per cent.

The authorities took advantage of the favorable circumstances to introduce structural reforms along the lines of the Italian and French examples at that time. As a first step, the banks were partially freed from the requirement that they hold cash and government securities equivalent to 65 per cent of their liabilities: at the end of 1961, any increases in deposits above the 1961 base were to be exempted. The banks were also permitted to reduce their holdings of short-term Treasury certificates, and their switches into longer-term bonds contributed to a further decline in security yields.

This step was followed in 1962 by a program under which their outstanding holdings of short debt were converted into nonnegotiable Treasury bonds in a three-stage operation. From January 1963 reserve requirements of government securities against deposits were abolished altogether.

Return to Credit Restraint

Aggregate demand increased strongly in Belgium, and credit expansion was quite rapid in 1963 and early 1964. The discount rate was raised in July and again in October. A speedup of public investment created a large budget deficit during 1963. But the Treasury covered nearly 60 per cent of its enlarged cash needs abroad—that is, the banks borrowed abroad to take up Treasury paper denominated in foreign currencies.

The central bank moved more vigorously in 1964. Credit ceilings were imposed: an agreement was concluded with the credit institutions to limit expansion of private loans to 10-12 per cent, about half the rate of increase in 1963. When the banks exceeded the established limits, the central bank imposed a 1 per cent non-interest-bearing reserve requirement in August. It also raised the discount rate and tightened eligibility requirements for rediscounting commercial paper.

These measures were very effective in checking the rate of credit expansion, and a temporary easing of credit took place during 1965. The business expansion began to taper off during 1964, and the index of industrial production flattened out in mid-1965. The balance of payments was in substantial surplus. In this environment the credit position was relaxed. In January 1965 rediscount terms were eased. Ceilings on bank loans and the 1 per cent penalty reserve were both rescinded in July.

However, this respite proved to be only temporary. Even though production showed very little growth after early 1965, the authorities were troubled by the rapid increases in wage rates and in consumer prices. Hence, they reactivated the ceilings on bank loans at the end of April, and in early May the government announced a package of stabilization measures which included a three-month freeze on prices of goods and services and a declaration that the rate of expansion of public spending would be slowed down. In June the discount rate was again advanced.

The swing of the German economy into recession late in 1966 and the slowdown in business activity in other countries of the Common Market also affected Belgium. As a result, the central bank eased credit policy gradually but actively during 1967, bringing down the discount rate from 5¼ to 4 per cent in five steps between February and October.

III. CREDIT POLICY AND THE BALANCE OF PAYMENTS

Between 1958 and 1967 the central banks in the countries in the European Economic Community acted contrary to the recommendations of an influential body of economic theorists in that they chose, in a system of fixed exchange rates and capital mobility, to direct monetary policy primarily to maintain internal balance.[27] They were chiefly preoccupied with their domestic responsibilities and used their powers and ingenuity to this end. One result was, from an historical point of view, a material enrichment of the craft of central banking.

But the burden of domestic stabilization was borne by credit policy with only "limited success," in Baffi's judgment, as measured by advances in domestic prices, in developments in the labor market, and in fluctuations in the balance of payments in the countries in the European Economic Community.[28] Baffi was quick to point out that the "monetary climate" in the Common Market was set by the more expansive policies of the three largest continental Western European countries, which chose, at least after the German and Dutch revaluations in 1961, "to reinforce external liquidity creation by domestic

[27] The literature on various aspects of monetary and fiscal mix under various exchange-rate systems includes: Robert A. Mundell, "The Appropriate Use of Monetary and Fiscal Policy for Internal and External Stability," International Monetary Fund *Staff Papers*, Vol. IX (March 1962), pp. 70-79; "The Monetary Dynamics of International Adjustment under Fixed and Flexible Exchange Rates," *Quarterly Journal of Economics*, Vol. LXXIV (May 1960), pp. 227-57; "Flexible Exchange Rates and Employment Policy," *Canadian Journal of Economics and Political Science*, Vol. 27 (November 1961), pp. 509-17; and "Capital Mobility and Stabilization Policy under Fixed and Flexible Exchange Rates," *ibid.*, Vol. 29 (November 1963), pp. 475-85; J. Marcus Fleming, "Domestic Financial Policies under Fixed and under Floating Exchange Rates," International Monetary Fund *Staff Papers*, Vol. IX (September 1962), pp. 369-80; Harry G. Johnson, "Some Aspects of the Theory of Economic Policy in a World of Capital Mobility," in *Essays in Honour of Marco Fanno* (Padova: Cedan, 1966), pp. 345-59; Egon Sohmen, "Fiscal and Monetary Policies under Alternative Exchange-Rate Systems," *Quarterly Journal of Economics*, Vol. LXXXI (August 1967), pp. 515-23; Anne O. Krueger, "The Impact of Alternative Government Policies under Varying Exchange Systems," *ibid.*, Vol. LXXIX (May 1965), pp. 195-208; David J. and Attiat F. Ott, "Monetary and Fiscal Policy: Goals and the Choice of Instruments," *ibid.*, Vol. LXXXII (May 1968), pp. 313-25; and Ronald I. McKinnon and Wallace E. Oates, *The Implications of International Economic Integration for Monetary, Fiscal, and Exchange-Rate Policy*, Princeton Studies in International Finance No. 16 (Princeton, N.J.: International Finance Section, 1966).

[28] Paolo Baffi, "The Inflation Problem in Europe," in *Inflation and Economic Policy* (New York: Model, Roland and Company, September 22, 1966), especially pp. 22-26. Dr. Baffi is General Manager of the Bank of Italy.

credit expansion."[29] This credit creation was not the involuntary consequences of technical limitations to the effectiveness of central-bank action, as Lutz and others had suggested they would be, but was a voluntary policy choice. For technical considerations such as "asset structure and institutional limitations to the implementation of restrictive policies would not have really prevented the adoption of a more severe policy line if in the judgment of the monetary authorities the situation had called for it."[30] Baffi was convinced that the range of new policy tools available to central banks would merely "have been advanced in time."

He divided the countries of the Common Market into those which:

(a) Offset the external liquidity—Germany and the Netherlands, from 1958 to 1961, achieved neutralization largely through the cash surpluses of the public sector,[31]

(b) Avoided secondary domestic liquidity creation—the Netherlands after 1961 no longer attempted to offset the primary effects of the surpluses,

(c) Permitted domestic credit creation—France, Italy, and Germany (after 1961) accepted the creation of secondary credit which reinforced the effects of the payments surpluses on their economies.

But the variations in the effectiveness of credit policy within the balance-of-payments cycle of each country may be a more rewarding focus for analysis than intercountry comparisons. Not only are these countries "open" to external developments, but their payments surpluses, especially between 1958 and 1961, were very large. From 1959 to 1961 the combined current-account surpluses of these five countries as a group averaged 2 per cent of GNP[32]; in terms of aggregates of the United States, a current-account surplus of around $16 billion would be implied.

EXTERNAL SURPLUSES AND DOMESTIC INFLATION

Baffi's judgment that credit policies could have been more stringent, had the central banks so decided, suggests that European monetary

[29] *Ibid.*, p. 29.

[30] Paolo Baffi, "Western European Inflation and the Reserve Currencies," *Banca Nazionale del Lavoro Quarterly Review*, No. 84 (March 1968), p. 11.

[31] He considers the revaluations of the Deutsche mark and the guilder in 1961 to be "perfectly consistent" with the neutralization policy. ("The Inflation Problem in Europe," *op.cit.*, p. 28.)

[32] See Table 7.

actions were not the unavoidable result of external monetary factors beyond the control of the central banks, but were instead largely determined by policy. If the monetary authorities were reasonably satisfied that additional restraint was not required, in spite of their purchases of inflowing foreign currencies, it is not an implausible inference to suggest that the sources of the disturbances to internal economic balance in the countries in the European Economic Community did not come directly from an undesired expansion in basic monetary aggregates.

Even though the overall external surplus may not have given rise to unwanted domestic liquidity in these countries, there still remains a potent, externally caused, source of internal business expansion. Changes in the export surplus plus net direct foreign investment impinge directly upon the output of goods and services. In a period of full employment, rapid growth, and optimistic entrepreneurial expectations, the European Economic Community's current-account surpluses and capital imports accelerated the expansion of domestic income and also helped to set off wage spirals as a result of excessive demands on European labor markets—a process largely outside the range of direct effectiveness of monetary measures.

Measurement of the effects of these surpluses on the process of income expansion requires models of the five economies of the Common Market which we do not have at hand. Both the magnitude of sectoral changes and the time-lags in this process, as would be found in the United States, can be reproduced by means of a simulation exercise based on the Federal Reserve-M.I.T. model of the American economy. In this model, an increase in exports would have about the same effect as the step increase in defense spending which is shown in Chart 9 on page 29.[33] In that simulation, an addition of $5 billion to defense spending produces—over a period of twelve quarters—an increase in GNP of roughly $16 billion: GNP reaches its peak in quarters five to eight; investment its peak in quarters four to six; and consumption spending its peak in quarter eleven, nearly three years later. In this model, an export expansion would have about the same effect on domestic fixed investment as a comparable step-up in defense spending, and a slightly reduced effect on inventories.

Without in any way implying that the time lags and sectoral changes in the countries in the European Economic Community are comparable

[33] Frank de Leeuw and Edward Gramlich, "The Federal Reserve–MIT Econometric Model," *Federal Reserve Bulletin*, Vol. 54 (January 1968), p. 11.

to those derived from a simulation of the American economy, it would seem evident that lags undoubtedly exist in those economies, too. If they do, then the abrupt growth in the Common Market's surplus on goods, services, and private unilateral transfers from an average of $630 million in the two years 1956 and 1957 to one of $2.5 billion for the four years 1958 through 1961 would remain an internal expansionary factor within those economies, even after the current-account surplus had been reduced in 1962 (see Table 5).

TABLE 5

EUROPEAN ECONOMIC COMMUNITY: SUMMARY BALANCE OF PAYMENTS,
ANNUAL AVERAGES FOR PERIOD, 1956 TO 1966
(in millions of dollars)

	1956-57	1958-61	1962-66
Goods, services, and private unilateral transfers	630	2,510	1,560
Official unilateral transfers	} —766	— 760	—1,020
Official capital		— 690	— 420
Prepayment of official debt	0	— 350	— 315
Direct investment	} 152	50	500
Other private long-term capital		780	815
Net military transactions	—a	895	34
Non-bank short-term capital and errors and omissions	321	— 145	— 290
Balance on non-monetary transactions	337b	2,290	1,170
Financing			
Change in official reserves	368b	2,330	1,270
Short-term banking flows	—150	— 40	— 100

a Not separately available for these years.

b Does not add because, in French accounts, transactions between the overseas franc area and the non-franc area affected through banks and other institutions in France (thus affecting French monetary reserves) have been excluded so that the totals will not balance out.

SOURCE: 1958 to 1966, U.S. Treasury Department, *Maintaining the Strength of the U.S. Dollar in a Strong Free World Economy*, January 1968, Table 22, p. 118; and for 1956 to 1957, International Monetary Fund.

The 1958-61 surpluses, because they occurred in a period of overfull employment, also set into motion a secondary process of wage-price inflation in these countries: the excess pressure on the labor market produced a wage "explosion" in Italy in 1962-63 and in the Netherlands in 1963-64, and less explosive but continuing wage-price spirals in the other three countries. The momentum of this spiral is illustrated by the Italian experience where wages continued to advance for nearly a year after Italian industrial production had dipped late in 1963. The lengthy period of wage contracts, the periodic bargaining sessions, and the time required for intersectoral wage adjustments to be completed help to explain why wages can continue to advance even after an initial stimulus of demand has subsided. Because of this protracted process, it is never easy *suddenly* to bring the spiral to a halt without drastic action such as a wage freeze.

An additional consideration should be noted. Even though the capital expenditures of enterprises, and not the external financing of direct investment, contribute to inflation, a sharp jump in foreign direct investment into the countries in the European Economic Community occurred in the period from 1962 to 1966 after the current account had begun to diminish. These inflows certainly helped to maintain the momentum of the internal investment booms in these countries, which was the principal stimulative factor in the German economy in this period and an important one elsewhere in the Common Market.

PAYMENTS DEFICITS AND MONETARY POLICY

The effectiveness of action by the central bank in a period of payments deficit differed in the countries in the European Economic Community from its effectiveness in a period of payments surplus. With a deficit, the central bank's control over domestic liquidity would be strengthened because the drain in liquidity from the banking system and from the private sector would eventually force the banks to seek accommodation from the central bank. The central bank might indeed find itself with some flexibility in policy-making. That is, the monetary authority would be able to choose from among a variety of policy actions, some of which could be selected to produce restraint (to correct the deficit) and others to produce some easing of liquidity pressures (to cushion the process of domestic adjustment) in a combination that would reconcile domestic economic priorities with the constraints of the balance of payments.

The added effectiveness of credit policy in a period of external deficit and domestic inflation must be regarded as the expected outcome of a situation in which the European central banks experienced no conflict between external and domestic policy. Once this conflict no longer existed, these banks were able to focus the instruments of credit policy upon the restraint of domestic demand. These credit actions, together with other elements of the government's stabilization effort, achieved a speedy rectification of the payments deficits in these countries between 1958 and 1966, as the experiences of Germany (1965-66), Italy (1963-64), France (1963 and 1966), the Netherlands (1964), and Belgium (1963-64) demonstrate (see Table 6). The rapid correction of the payments deficits of individual members also contributed to the strength of the European Economic Community's combined international position. As a group, the Common Market's current account swung from a large surplus in the second half of 1961 to an equivalent surplus three years later (late 1964) and again in the second half of 1967 (see Table 6). Actual deficits on current account were recorded only in the first halves of 1963 and 1964 and the first quarter of 1966. The rapidity with which the current account could be swung around in each partner country must have contributed to Baffi's general satisfaction with the capabilities of European central banks to make credit policy effective.

PAYMENTS SURPLUSES AND DOMESTIC INFLATION

By contrast, these central banks found that, in periods of external surpluses, the commercial banks were less dependent upon them; in addition, the authorities often faced a grave conflict between international and domestic policy demands. As a result, the European banks either instituted credit rationing or arranged for the banking system to place excess liquidity abroad.

But in these circumstances, credit policy alone was not adequate for the job of domestic liquidity restraint, and the European officials turned to technical Treasury financial operations (both debt- and cash-management) to support the efforts of the central bank. These Treasury operations, which were helpful even in circumstances where current public-sector spending was adding to total demand, can be grouped under three general headings:

(a) Domestic debt repayment—Long-term borrowings could be used to repay short-term Treasury debt held by the bank or, even more effective, by the central bank;

(b) Foreign debt repayments, prepayments, foreign credits, reparations, and Treasury purchases abroad—The variety and magnitude of these external transactions, all of which had deflationary domestic effects, were unprecedented in the period under review;

37

TABLE 6

COUNTRIES OF THE EUROPEAN ECONOMIC COMMUNITY:
CURRENT-ACCOUNT BALANCES, QUARTERLY, 1961 TO 1967
(in millions of dollars)

	Germany¹	Italy	France	Netherlands	Belgium	Total
1961: I	(484) 470	—88	513	54	—38	1,108
II	(425) 217	44		—64		
III	(478) 39	329	459	139	128	1,226
IV	(286) 24	78		30		
1962: I	(130) —49	—29	239	—33	62	407
II	(130) —65	13	311	—42		
III	(262) —140	328	209	123	20	430
IV	(225) —133	—182	69	136		
1963: I	(171) —79	—194	147	—8	6	—308
II	(284) —80	—218	181	—63		
III	(299) —141	—24	163	108	—88	382
IV	(715) 520	—269	20	45		
1964: I	(526) 307	—448	—65	—149	—72	—452
II	(472) 118	18	68	—229		
III	(119) —261	689	57	88	70	1,163
IV	(211) —44	426	27	111		
1965: I	(263) —58	262	109	10	134	459
II	(—53) —645	556	178	—87		
III	(—120) —655	876	180	148	18	985
IV	(181) —160	542	51	—15		
1966: I	(120) —293	219	95	—210	—8	197
II	(279) —146	565	146	—90	0	475
III	(575) 49	928	—92	93	—46	932
IV	(881) 497	405	—116	60	—18	828
1967: I	(1,027) 667	183	—70	—80	86	786
II	(1,070) 627	448	—48	—87	50	990
III	(976) 369	786	—2	132	18	1,303
IV	(1,088) 751	282	22	—11	40	1,084

¹ Because official German transfers abroad during this period were so substantial, Germany's trade balance (on a c.i.f. basis) is shown in parentheses for comparative purposes.

source: International Monetary Fund

(c) Accumulating Treasury balances at the central bank—This buildup of official deposits was at the expense of commercial-bank liquidity.

SOURCES OF INFLATION: EXTERNAL OR DOMESTIC?

After 1961 the trade surpluses of the European Economic Community receded, and the pace of internal inflation quickened. These diverging trends have led some observers to minimize the external influences on Europe's inflation between 1960 and 1966. The Bank for International Settlements, for example, has concluded that "as Europe's exports to outside areas ceased to expand after 1960, the emergence of inflation in 1962-63 cannot be attributed to the direct influence of the over-all account surplus."[34]

Baffi concluded similarly that "the movement of prices was to a large extent governed by changes of domestic origin in the volume of demand."[35] To measure the impact of impulses from abroad, he made year-by-year comparisons between the rate of price increases and the the domestic origin of inflation is based, again, on the declining trend current-account surplus (as a proportion of GNP). His emphasis on in the current account, coinciding with a rising price trend (see Table 7). He goes on to describe a "familiar . . . process of overheating, in

TABLE 7

EUROPEAN ECONOMIC COMMUNITY: COMPARISON OF PRICE
INCREASES AND COMBINED CURRENT-ACCOUNT SURPLUSES, 1959 TO 1966

	Annual rate of price increase	Current account (as % of GNP)
1959	2.5	2.5
1960	2.7	2.1
1961	3.6	1.5
Average (1959-61)	2.9	2.0
Average (1962-66)	4.2	0.7

SOURCE: Paolo Baffi, "Western European Inflation and The Reserve Currencies," *Banca Nazionale del Lavoro Quarterly Review*, No. 84 (March 1968), pp. 14-15.

[34] Bank for International Settlements, *Thirty-Fourth Annual Report*, 1963-1964, p. 8.
[35] Baffi, "Western European Inflation and the Reserve Currencies," *op.cit.*, p. 16.

which an expansion in investment demand or in government consumption leads to a wage explosion followed by a downward adjustment. Memorable experiences were those in Italy in 1963-1964, the Netherlands and Germany in 1964-1966."[36]

But this emphasis upon the domestic origin of inflationary impulses appears seriously to underestimate the *delayed* effects of Europe's current-account surpluses in at least three respects. In the first place, this analysis, which is based on year-by-year movements of price and foreign trade, fails to recognize the time lags for the external impulses to work themselves out within the European economies. Clearly, two separate time paths of response were involved:

(a) From the spurt in export demand to the peak in investment and then in consumer demand generated by the additional exports; and

(b) From the overheating of the labor market, once it is set off by excess demand, to the eventual crest of the wage spiral.

To expect domestic effects of either of these cycles to be completed within the year in which the spurt in exports occurs would seem to be unrealistic.

Second, the integration of the countries in the Economic European Community has increased the "spill over" of excess demand from country to country. Attempts to achieve domestic balance could be disturbed, not only by a spurt in export sales outside the Community, but from additional demands for imports or for manpower from partner countries. The expansion in German exports in 1963-64 can be attributed to Italian and French "excess" demand, just as the wage "explosion" in the Netherlands in late 1963 was accelerated by demands for Dutch manpower, especially from Germany. Because the European Economic Community as a unit was in almost continuous surplus in this period, one or more countries usually had an appreciable payments surplus, creating additional demand pressures on partner countries in the Community (see Table 6).

Finally, the conflict between domestic and international objectives, which became more acute as capital mobility increased, forced the European central banks to make compromises in planning the strategy of monetary policy. It is too literal a conception to limit the influences of external factors to the actual movements of goods and capital; allowance must also be made for the extent that central banks on occasion

[36] *Loc.cit.*

40

limited their domestic credit actions to avoid provoking inflows of capital from abroad.

CREDIT POLICY AND THE ADJUSTMENT MECHANISM

The European central banks did learn to cope with the international movements of capital which actually took place. In the first place, special incentives to have the excess liquidity placed abroad were effective in the German experience in enabling the central bank to retain control of the internal credit base, even in a period of external surplus. In addition, these outflows of capital had the very important temporary effect of returning to the international financial system the reserves being drained into Germany.

But this measure was also disruptive to the attainment of external balance to the extent that it interfered with the longer-run processes of payments adjustment. As Brehmer pointed out in his seminal study of German official forward-exchange operations, the monetary authorities, through the use of forward operations, can "maintain domestic interest rates that are higher or lower than those prevailing in foreign money markets, and this can be done without inducing international movements of capital."[37] The short-run effects on the balance of payments of changing the costs of forward cover to the banks is "essentially the same as those of equivalent variations in domestic interest rates," but the long-run effects are different. For "a lowering of interest rates will stimulate an expansion of the domestic economy and, in the long run, will induce a reduction in the balance of payments on current account. Such an effect cannot be expected from forward operations."[38]

Second, the European central banks increased their use of controls over international capital movements, especially in the inward direction, to supplement measures taken to induce outflows of capital. Limitations were placed on the ways foreigners could put their funds in local money markets. In Italy and France, the money markets are essentially interbank markets, and in Germany and Belgium, foreigners were prohibited from buying short-term Government securities;

[37] Ekhard Brehmer, "Official Forward Exchange Operations: The German Experience," International Monetary Fund *Staff Papers*, Vol. XI (November 1964), p. 389.

[38] *Ibid.*, p. 390. "On the contrary," he added, "if the current account balance should be affected by the slight depreciation of the domestic currency that is implied in the lowering of the forward rate, the result would be an increase (likely to be negligible) in the balance."

hence, nonresidents tended to place time deposits with local banks until regulations in Germany and France prohibited the payment of interest on such accounts. The freedom of residents in France, the Netherlands, and to a lesser extent Italy, to borrow abroad was also narrowly circumscribed by regulation.

The momentum toward the selective regulation of capital flows has since accelerated outside the Common Market, particularly with regard to capital regulations by the United States and United Kingdom to reduce their external payments deficits. These measures have helped provide the countries in the Common Market an additional degree of freedom for domestic credit actions without "interference" from international movements of funds. This gradual drift away from the degree of currency convertibility which had been achieved by 1960 can be directly attributed to the desire of the monetary authorities in Western countries to weaken the link between flows of capital and internal money-market and credit conditions.

IV. CONCLUDING OBSERVATIONS

Adaptations in the techniques of central banking over the past ten years represent attempts by European officials to maintain control over key internal credit aggregates in the unpromising conditions of domestic boom and continuing external surpluses. As such, these new tools constitute a material enrichment of the craft of central banking, even though some of them emerged as *ad hoc* responses to difficulties, sometimes even through a process of trial and error. In a world of better domestic economic balance and better processes of international adjustment than we have experienced since 1958, the central banks might find the need for some of these new techniques diminished and allow them to fall into disuse. In such a world, in fact, the European central banks might be able to return to a traditional emphasis on the discount rate and uniform reserve requirements as primary tools of control. But even in those circumstances some of the new practices would undoubtedly survive.

In a world of external and internal imbalances on the scale experienced in recent years, however, these new policy instruments were indispensable. Without them, European officials could not have realized their determination to discharge their primary responsibility for internal stability, even where external factors threatened the central bank's control over the domestic credit situation. With them, the central banks were able to make monetary policy the principal instrument of domestic stabilization in these countries, often with only limited support from fiscal policy, during this period.

Two observations need to be made about the domestic focus of central-banking policy in this period. In the first place, the European central banks were not altogether successful in maintaining internal stability in the face of continuing external surpluses, as the advances of prices and wages after 1960 indicate. Each of the countries in the Common Market experienced a period of current-account deficit between 1963 and 1966 (see Table 6). Once the external surplus had been eliminated, however, the domestic and external objectives of credit policy were more easily reconciled; in those circumstances, monetary policy could play a major role in the effort for stabilization which, in each case, rapidly wiped out the current-account deficit.[39]

[39] From this European experience, Emminger has suggested that "where a serious attempt was made to eliminate a big external deficit by restraining domestic

This speedy rectification of external deficits was one of the major achievements of the European authorities between 1958 and 1966.

Second, the European central banks sought primarily to attain domestic economic goals, even when such policies conflicted with the requirements of international balance. As a result, we find general tendencies, both in Europe and outside, toward the use of direct controls to check international flows of capital and, thereby, to break the link between domestic and international financial markets in the major industrial countries. This process of economic fragmentation, accompanied in the recent period by repeated international financial disturbances, reflects largely the absence of any agreed path of balance-of-payments adjustment among the countries of the Group of Ten. This absence can be attributed in part to the subordination of international to domestic economic objectives, both in Europe and elsewhere, and in part to the use of offsetting techniques which reduce the impact of "automatic" corrective forces in the world payments system.

Mundell has pointed out that "The decline of automaticity [in the international adjustment mechanism] dates from the first attempts of central banks to adjust the domestic supply of notes to accord with the needs of trade (the banking principle) instead of the requirements of external equilibrium (the bullionist principle)."[40] This break in the link between the balance of payments and the money supply constitutes the heart of what he terms the *international disequilibrium system.*

That central bankers in our generation have not been prepared to watch passively as international influences disturb the internal economy without regard to domestic priorities ought not require comment. Acceptance of Mundell's plea for "consistent instruments of equilibration"[41] would, in a world of fixed (that is, virtually unchanging) exchange rates, impose on central banks the goal of external balance as the overriding objective of monetary action. Such a develop-

---

demand, the adjustment mechanism nearly always worked with astonishing speed and vigor." See Otmar Emminger, "Practical Aspects of the Problem of Balance-of-Payments Adjustment," *Journal of Political Economy,* Vol. 75 (Supplement: August 1967), p. 522. However, the cases he cites are instances where the domestic and external objectives of policy were consistent; the difficult cases of international economic adjustment are, of course, the ones where those objectives are in direct conflict.

[40] Robert A. Mundell, "The International Disequilibrium System," *Kyklos,* Vol. 14, No. 2 (1961), p. 153.

[41] *Ibid.,* p. 153, n. 2.

ment would be a massive step in the direction of restoring the non-discretionary, automatic character of the world gold standard, as it actually (or should have) operated before 1913.

Such limitations on the scope of discretionary monetary action by the central bank are not consistent with contemporary notions about the use of policy tools to maintain sustainable domestic economic expansion. It would also be, from an historical point of view, a retrograde step. Since the Bretton Woods Agreement in 1944, nations have been unwilling to accept international economic arrangements that place upon each country's domestic economy the full burden of automatic adjustment to external disturbance in all circumstances. International agreement on this point was, in fact, one of the historic accomplishments of that Conference.

This historic shift in thinking helps to explain why European central bankers between 1958 and 1966 felt impelled to make individual decisions about how far they were prepared to permit domestic expansion to proceed during a period of external surplus and then set about—admittedly with varying degrees of success—to translate those decisions into effective action. This approach should be faulted not because it is a break with the Hume adjustment process, but because the countries of the Group of Ten have not made policy adjustments elsewhere to maintain external payments balance, once they had determined to use monetary policy chiefly for internal objectives. The absence of such adjustments—the lack of agreement on workable arrangements for restoring international payments balance between the two sides of the North Atlantic Community—remains the principal threat to the continuance of the reconstructed arrangements for liberal trade and payments which must surely rank as one of the Free World's major international achievements in the era following World War II.

PUBLICATIONS OF THE
INTERNATIONAL FINANCE SECTION

The International Finance Section publishes at irregular intervals papers in four series: ESSAYS IN INTERNATIONAL FINANCE, PRINCETON STUDIES IN INTERNATIONAL FINANCE, SPECIAL PAPERS IN INTERNATIONAL ECONOMICS, and REPRINTS IN INTERNATIONAL FINANCE. All four of these should be ordered directly from the Section (P.O. Box 644, Princeton, New Jersey 08540).

A mailing list is maintained for free distribution of ESSAYS and REPRINTS as they are issued and of announcements of new issues in the series of STUDIES and SPECIAL PAPERS. Requests for inclusion in this list will be honored, except that students will not be placed on the permanent mailing list, because waste results from frequent changes of address.

For the STUDIES and SPECIAL PAPERS there will be a charge of $1.00 a copy, payable in advance. This charge will be waived on copies distributed to college and university libraries here and abroad. In addition the charge is sometimes waived on single copies requested by persons residing abroad who find it difficult to make remittance.

For noneducational institutions there is a simplified procedure whereby all issues of all four series will be sent to them automatically in return for a contribution of $25 to the publication program of the International Finance Section. Any company finding it irksome to order individual SPECIAL PAPERS and STUDIES is welcome to take advantage of this plan.

Orders for single copies of the ESSAYS and REPRINTS will be filled against a handling charge of $1.00, payable in advance. The charge for more than one copy of these two series will be $0.50 a copy. These charges may be waived to foreign institutions of education and research. Charges may also be waived on single copies requested by persons residing abroad who find it difficult to make remittance.

For the convenience of our British customers, arrangements have been made for retail distribution of the STUDIES and SPECIAL PAPERS through the Economists' Bookshop, Portugal Street, London, W.C. 2, and Blackwells, Broad Street, Oxford. These booksellers will usually have our publications in stock.

The following is a complete list of the publications of the International Finance Section. The issues of the four series that are still available from the Section are marked by asterisks. Those marked by daggers are out of stock at the International Finance Section but may be obtained in xerographic reproductions (that is, looking like the originals) from University Microfilm, Inc., 300 N. Zeeb Road, Ann Arbor, Michigan 48106. (Most of the issues are priced at $3.00.)

46

†No. 1. Friedrich A. Lutz, *International Monetary Mechanisms: The Keynes and White Proposals.* (July 1943)

† 2. Frank D. Graham, *Fundamentals of International Monetary Policy.* (Autumn 1943)

† 3. Richard A. Lester, *International Aspects of Wartime Monetary Experience.* (Aug. 1944)

† 4. Ragnar Nurkse, *Conditions of International Monetary Equilibrium.* (Spring 1945)

† 5. Howard S. Ellis, *Bilateralism and the Future of International Trade.* (Summer 1945)

† 6. Arthur I. Bloomfield, *The British Balance-of-Payments Problem.* (Autumn 1945)

† 7. Frank A. Southard, Jr., *Some European Currency and Exchange Experiences: 1943-1946.* (Summer 1946)

† 8. Miroslav A. Kriz, *Postwar International Lending.* (Spring 1947)

† 9. Friedrich A. Lutz, *The Marshall Plan and European Economic Policy.* (Spring 1948)

† 10. Frank D. Graham, *The Cause and Cure of "Dollar Shortage."* (Jan. 1949)

† 11. Horst Mendershausen, *Dollar Shortage and Oil Surplus in 1949-1950.* (Nov. 1950)

† 12. Sir Arthur Salter, *Foreign Investment.* (Feb. 1951)

† 13. Sir Roy Harrod, *The Pound Sterling.* (Feb. 1952)

† 14. S. Herbert Frankel, *Some Conceptual Aspects of International Economic Development of Underdeveloped Territories.* (May 1952)

† 15. Miroslav A. Kriz, *The Price of Gold.* (July 1952)

† 16. William Diebold, Jr., *The End of the I.T.O.* (Oct. 1952)

† 17. Sir Douglas Copland, *Problems of the Sterling Area: With Special Reference to Australia.* (Sept. 1953)

† 18. Raymond F. Mikesell, *The Emerging Pattern of International Payments.* (April 1954)

† 19. D. Gale Johnson, *Agricultural Price Policy and International Trade.* (June 1954)

† 20. Ida Greaves, "The Colonial Sterling Balances." (Sept. 1954)

† 21. Raymond Vernon, *America's Foreign Trade Policy and the GATT.* (Oct. 1954)

† 22. Roger Auboin, *The Bank for International Settlements, 1930-1955.* (May 1955)

† 23. Wytze Gorter, *United States Merchant Marine Policies: Some International Implications.* (June 1955)

† 24. Thomas C. Schelling, *International Cost-Sharing Arrangements.* (Sept. 1955)

† 25. James E. Meade, *The Belgium-Luxembourg Economic Union, 1921-1939.* (March 1956)

† 26. Samuel I. Katz, *Two Approaches to the Exchange-Rate Problem: The United Kingdom and Canada.* (Aug. 1956)

† 27. A. R. Conan, *The Changing Pattern of International Investment in Selected Sterling Countries.* (Dec. 1956)

† 28. Fred H. Klopstock, *The International Status of the Dollar.* (May 1957)

† 29. Raymond Vernon, *Trade Policy in Crisis.* (March 1958)

† 30. Sir Roy Harrod, *The Pound Sterling, 1951-1958.* (Aug. 1958)

† 31. Randall Hinshaw, *Toward European Convertibility.* (Nov. 1958)

† 32. Francis H. Schott, *The Evolution of Latin American Exchange-Rate Policies since World War II.* (Jan. 1959)

† 33. Alec Cairncross, *The International Bank for Reconstruction and Development.* (March 1959)

† 34. Miroslav A. Kriz, *Gold in World Monetary Affairs Today.* (June 1959)

† 35. Sir Donald MacDougall, *The Dollar Problem: A Reappraisal.* (Nov. 1960)
† 36. Brian Tew, *The International Monetary Fund: Its Present Role and Future Prospect.* (March 1961)
† 37. Samuel I. Katz, *Sterling Speculation and European Convertibility: 1955-1958.* (Oct. 1961)
† 38. Boris C. Swerling, *Current Issues in International Commodity Policy.* (June 1962)
† 39. Pieter Lieftinck, *Recent Trends in International Monetary Policies.* (Sept. 1962)
† 40. Jerome L. Stein, *The Nature and Efficiency of the Foreign Exchange Market.* (Oct. 1962)
† 41. Friedrich A. Lutz, *The Problem of International Liquidity and the Multiple-Currency Standard.* (March 1963)
† 42. Sir Dennis Robertson, *A Memorandum Submitted to the Canadian Royal Commission on Banking and Finance.* (May 1963)
† 43. Marius W. Holtrop, *Monetary Policy in an Open Economy: Its Objectives, Instruments, Limitations, and Dilemmas.* (Sept. 1963)
† 44. Harry G. Johnson, *Alternative Guiding Principles for the Use of Monetary Policy.* (Nov. 1963)
† 45. Jacob Viner, *Problems of Monetary Control.* (May 1964)
† 46. Charles P. Kindleberger, *Balance-of-Payments Deficits and the International Market for Liquidity.* (May 1965)
† 47. Jacques Rueff and Fred Hirsch, *The Role and the Rule of Gold: An Argument.* (June 1965)
† 48. Sidney Weintraub, *The Foreign-Exchange Gap of the Developing Countries.* (Sept. 1965)
† 49. Tibor Scitovsky, *Requirements of an International Reserve System.* (Nov. 1965)
† 50. John H. Williamson, *The Crawling Peg.* (Dec. 1965)
† 51. Pieter Lieftinck, *External Debt and Debt-Bearing Capacity of Developing Countries.* (March 1966)
† 52. Raymond F. Mikesell, *Public Foreign Capital for Private Enterprise in Developing Countries.* (April 1966)
† 53. Milton Gilbert, *Problems of the International Monetary System.* (April 1966)
† 54. Robert V. Roosa and Fred Hirsch, *Reserves, Reserve Currencies, and Vehicle Currencies: An Argument.* (May 1966)
† 55. Robert Triffin, *The Balance of Payments and the Foreign Investment Position of the United States.* (Sept. 1966)
† 56. John Parke Young, *United States Gold Policy: The Case for Change.* (Oct. 1966)
* 57. Gunther Ruff, *A Dollar-Reserve System as a Transitional Solution.* (Jan. 1967)
* 58. J. Marcus Fleming, *Toward Assessing the Need for International Reserves.* (Feb. 1967)
* 59. N. T. Wang, *New Proposals for the International Finance of Development.* (April 1967)
† 60. Miroslav A. Kriz, *Gold: Barbarous Relic or Useful Instrument?* (June 1967)
* 61. Charles P. Kindleberger, *The Politics of International Money and World Language.* (Aug. 1967)
* 62. Delbert A. Snider, *Optimum Adjustment Processes and Currency Areas.* (Oct. 1967)
* 63. Eugene A. Birnbaum, *Changing the United States Commmitment to Gold.* (Nov. 1967)
* 64. Alexander K. Swoboda, *The Euro-Dollar Market: An Interpretation.* (Feb. 1968)
* 65. Fred H. Klopstock, *The Euro-Dollar Market: Some Unresolved Issues.* (March 1968)
* 66. Eugene A. Birnbaum, *Gold and the International Monetary System: An Orderly Reform.* (April 1968)

* 67. J. Marcus Fleming, *Guidelines for Balance-of-Payments Adjustment under the Par-Value System.* (May 1968)
* 68. George N. Halm, *International Financial Intermediation: Deficits Benign and Malignant.* (June 1968)
* 69. Albert O. Hirschman and Richard M. Bird, *Foreign Aid—A Critique and a Proposal.* (July 1968)
* 70. Milton Gilbert, *The Gold-Dollar System: Conditions of Equilibrium and the Price of Gold.* (Nov. 1968)
* 71. Henry G. Aubrey, *Behind the Veil of International Money.* (Jan. 1969)

PRINCETON STUDIES IN INTERNATIONAL FINANCE

†No. 1. Friedrich A. and Vera C. Lutz, *Monetary and Foreign Exchange Policy in Italy.* (Jan. 1950)
† 2. Eugene R. Schlesinger, *Multiple Exchange Rates and Economic Development.* (May 1952)
† 3. Arthur I. Bloomfield, *Speculative and Flight Movements of Capital in Postwar International Finance.* (Feb. 1954)
† 4. Merlyn N. Trued and Raymond F. Mikesell, *Postwar Bilateral Payments Agreements.* (April 1955)
† 5. Derek Curtis Bok, *The First Three Years of the Schuman Plan.* (Dec. 1955)
† 6. James E. Meade, *Negotiations for Benelux: An Annotated Chronicle, 1943-1956.* (March 1957)
† 7. H. H. Liesner, *The Import Dependence of Britain and Western Germany: A Comparative Study.* (Dec. 1957)
† 8. Raymond F. Mikesell and Jack N. Behrman, *Financing Free World Trade with the Sino-Soviet Bloc.* (Sept. 1958)
† 9. Marina von Neumann Whitman, *The United States Investment Guaranty Program and Private Foreign Investment.* (Dec. 1959)
† 10. Peter B. Kenen, *Reserve-Asset Preferences of Central Banks and Stability of the Gold-Exchange Standard.* (June 1963)
* 11. Arthur I. Bloomfield, *Short-Term Capital Movements under the Pre-1914 Gold Standard.* (July 1963)
* 12. Robert Triffin, *The Evolution of the International Monetary System: Historical Reappraisal and Future Perspectives.* (June 1964)
* 13. Robert Z. Aliber, *The Management of the Dollar in International Finance.* (June 1964)
* 14. Weir M. Brown, *The External Liquidity of an Advanced Country.* (Oct. 1964)
† 15. E. Ray Canterbery, *Foreign Exchange, Capital Flows, and Monetary Policy.* (June 1965)
* 16. Ronald I. McKinnon and Wallace E. Oates, *The Implications of International Economic Integration for Monetary, Fiscal, and Exchange-Rate Policy.* (March 1966)
* 17. Egon Sohmen, *The Theory of Forward Exchange.* (Aug. 1966)
* 18. Benjamin J. Cohen, *Adjustment Costs and the Distribution of New Reserves.* (Oct. 1966)
* 19. Marina von Neumann Whitman, *International and Interregional Payments Adjustment: A Synthetic View.* (Feb. 1967)
* 20. Fred R. Glahe, *An Empirical Study of the Foreign-Exchange Market: Test of A Theory.* (June 1967)
* 21. Arthur I. Bloomfield, *Patterns of Fluctuation in International Investment.* (Dec. 1968)
* 22. Samuel I. Katz, *External Surpluses, Capital Flows, and Credit Policy in the European Economic Community.* (Feb. 1969)

SPECIAL PAPERS IN INTERNATIONAL ECONOMICS

*No. 1. Gottfried Haberler, *A Survey of International Trade Theory.* (Sept. 1955; Revised edition, July 1961)
† 2. Oskar Morgenstern, *The Validity of International Gold Movement Statistics.* (Nov. 1955)
* 3. Fritz Machlup, *Plans for Reform of the International Monetary System.* (Aug. 1962; Revised edition, March 1964)

† 4. Egon Sohmen, *International Monetary Problems and the Foreign Exchanges.* (April 1963)

† 5. Walther Lederer, *The Balance on Foreign Transactions: Problems of Definition and Measurement.* (Sept. 1963)

* 6. George N. Halm, *The "Band" Proposal: The Limits of Permissible Exchange Rate Variations.* (Jan. 1965)

* 7. W. M. Corden, *Recent Developments in the Theory of International Trade.* (March 1965)

* 8. Jagdish Bhagwati, *The Theory and Practice of Commercial Policy: Departures from Unified Exchange Rates.* (Jan. 1968)

REPRINTS IN INTERNATIONAL FINANCE

†No. 1. Fritz Machlup, *The Cloakroom Rule of International Reserves: Reserve Creation and Resources Transfer.* [Reprinted from *Quarterly Journal of Economics*, Vol. LXXIX (Aug. 1965)]

† 2. Fritz Machlup, *Real Adjustment, Compensatory Corrections, and Foreign Financing of Imbalances in International Payments.* [Reprinted from Robert E. Baldwin *et al.*, *Trade, Growth, and the Balance of Payments* (Chicago: Rand McNally and Amsterdam: North-Holland Publishing Co., 1965)]

† 3. Fritz Machlup, *International Monetary Systems and the Free Market Economy.* [Reprinted from *International Payments Problems: A Symposium* (Washington, D.C.: American Enterprise Institute, 1966)]

* 4. Fritz Machlup, *World Monetary Debate—Bases for Agreement.* [Reprinted from *The Banker*, Vol. 116 (Sept. 1966)]

* 5. Fritz Machlup, *The Need for Monetary Reserves.* [Reprinted from *Banca Nazionale del Lavoro Quarterly Review*, Vol. 77 (Sept. 1966)]

* 6. Benjamin J. Cohen, *Voluntary Foreign Investment Curbs: A Plan that Really Works.* [Reprinted from *Challenge: The Magazine of Economic Affairs* (March/April 1967)]

* 7. Fritz Machlup, *Credit Facilities or Reserve Allotments?* [Reprinted from *Banca Nazionale del Lavoro Quarterly Review*, No. 81 (June 1967)]

* 8. Fritz Machlup, *From Dormant Liabilities to Dormant Assets.* [Reprinted from *The Banker*, Vol. 117 (Sept. 1967)])

* 9. Benjamin J. Cohen, *Reparations in the Postwar Period: A Survey.* [Reprinted from *Banca Nazionale del Lavoro Quarterly Review*, No. 82 (Sept. 1967)]

* 10. Fritz Machlup, *The Price of Gold.* [Reprinted from *The Banker*, Vol. 118 (Sept. 1968)]

* 11. Fritz Machlup, *The Transfer Gap of the United States.* [Reprinted from *Banca Nazionale del Lavoro Quarterly Review*, No. 86 (Sept. 1968)]

SEPARATE PUBLICATIONS

† (1) Klaus Knorr and Gardner Patterson (editors), *A Critique of the Randall Commission Report.* (1954)

† (2) Gardner Patterson and Edgar S. Furniss Jr. (editors), *NATO: A Critical Appraisal.* (1957)

* (3) Fritz Machlup and Burton G. Malkiel (editors), *International Monetary Arrangements: The Problem of Choice.* Report on the Deliberations of an International Study Group of 32 Economists. (Aug. 1964) [$1.00]

AVAILABLE FROM OTHER SOURCES

William Fellner, Fritz Machlup, Robert Triffin, and Eleven Others, *Maintaining and Restoring Balance in International Payments* (1966). [This volume may be ordered from Princeton University Press, Princeton, New Jersey 08540, at a price of $6.50.]

Fritz Machlup, *Remaking the International Monetary System: The Rio Agreement and Beyond* (1968). [This volume may be ordered from the Johns Hopkins Press, Baltimore, Maryland 21218, at $6.95 in cloth cover and $2.45 in paperback.]

$1.00